The 17% Plan

Investing in Mutual Funds Wisely

by

Dennis E. Anstett

ISBN 0969922000

First printing, November 1994.
Second printing, December 1994.

Published by
Anstett Investments Inc.
RR #1
Wellesley, Ontario
N0B 2T0
Telephone: (519) 656-3565

There are over 850 mutual funds sold in Canada. The information in this book may not apply to all funds. Financial market movements are never a certainty. The publisher and author disclaim liability for any adverse circumstances that may result directly or indirectly from the use of this material.

To Sherry, who inspired me to take this step.

TABLE OF CONTENTS

ACKNOWLEDGEMENTS

Writing about a topic that enriches people's lives has been most fulfilling. The friendships and experiences will last a lifetime, and I have a new-found admiration for people who write for a living.

Without the support of those closest to me, the book would still be just a thought. My wife Sherry and children Jauna and Jarred deserve special recognition for all of their understanding, sacrifices and encouragement.

I also want to thank the people and financial institutions that I do business with. Your service has made this book a reality. To remain impartial, no names are mentioned. You know who you are.

Thank you to Diane Stoody for the design of the book cover and to Rosemary Voll for the layout of the book.

Some of the ideas and information in the book have come from articles read in The Calgary Herald, The Globe and Mail, The Financial Post, Henry Zimmer's *The Money Manager* and Jack D. Schwager's *The New Market Wizards*.

A final thank you must go to my parents, Thelma and Elroy, who taught me to always spend a little less than what I earn and invest the difference.

INTRODUCTION

I'll never forget my first experience with a financial planner. It was rather enlightening, to say the least. The guy had forgotten I already had a Registered Retirement Savings Plan, virtually ignored my questions about the investments he was recommending, and suggested I needed more life insurance. I suggested I didn't need his services.

The disappointing encounter actually turned into a blessing in disguise because I decided right then and there to take charge of my investment program myself.

What happened to many mutual fund investors in 1994 only reaffirmed that I made the right decision back in 1987. And it was one of the key reasons I wrote this book — to not only protect the consumer, but to help the investor get a higher rate of return.

Of the more than 850 mutual funds available in Canada in 1994, many lost money and a lot of the others barely broke even. The average rate of return was about one per cent. Some of the funds lost as much as 20 per cent. Using my safe, low-risk method of investing in mutual funds, I earned 18 per cent.

And, I'm happy to say, my older brother Larry did even better. Larry, who helped me put the finishing touches on the book, was formerly a writer and editor with the Kitchener-Waterloo Record until retiring in May of 1994 at age 43. Larry made the decision to quit a career he had loved for most of the 25 years based on two factors: Working the night shift had created a lifestyle he could no longer tolerate, and he was convinced he could live comfortably if he could get a rate of return similar to mine, as long as it wasn't too risky.

After I taught him what I knew, Larry's portfolio gained more than 30 per cent for the year. Larry took my system and adapted it to his more aggressive style, taking larger positions in the funds.

Clearly, this book is about moving your money around to get a higher rate of return. It's a philosophy that contradicts what is often advised — that when the markets go down, leave your money in and don't worry because the markets will eventually come back up. But the question is, when? And, is the buy-and-hold strategy the best way to invest when there is an alternative?

This book is also about a whole lot more. It's about protecting your money; it's about stuffing as much money as possible into RRSPs because the benefits are too fantastic to pass up; it's about diversifying your portfolio, but not over-diversifying; and it's about becoming an informed, curious investor, questioning a lot of what you hear and read, especially the value of dollar-cost averaging.

I've been doing all of this since 1987 and the result is what you see on the cover of this book — *The 17% Plan*. I've earned an average of 17 per cent on my money, which, in that time frame, has beaten just about every Canadian mutual fund. My average for the last five years is even better — 20 per cent. I point this out not to boast, but to show what's possible.

I should also mention that I started doing this at probably the worst time. Remember the Stock Market Crash of 1987? Sorry if I'm bringing up any bad memories, but by being in control of my money, I bailed out of the markets on the Friday, taking only a small loss before the roof caved in the following Monday. I wound up making 11 per cent that year.

Mutual funds have grown to be so sophisticated and diversified that it's possible to prevent yearly losses if you've got some basic knowledge of how the funds work. And I'm here to give you that knowledge. I've never had a negative year in my investing, and my lowest return was 7.5 per cent. That was in 1988 when there was still a lot of nervousness following The Crash. It was my only year below 10 per cent.

It may well be that you're happy with your rate of return and investment strategy. If so, great. But consider this: Many people bought mutual funds in early 1994 based on unusually high returns the previous year. And many of those people didn't really know what they were buying, so they were unprepared for what was about to hit them.

It's up to the consumer to be informed, and helping you become informed is what *The 17% Plan* is all about. Even if you're inclined to retain your current investment style, you'll still find this book invaluable because of its helpful, straight-forward information.

One of my old high school teachers said the reason we have two eyes, two ears and only one mouth is because we're supposed to look and listen twice as much as we talk. That's exactly what I did in the past number of years in my quest for knowledge about mutual funds, and it may be good advice for you as well, particularly if you're just starting out. Those of you willing to try the principles in this book have virtually nothing to lose and everything to gain. As the old saying goes: Try it, you may like it. A lot of my friends already love it.

If the thought of managing your own investments is a little scary, remember this: You're adjusting to new and seemingly complicated things every day of your life. Many of you now have microwaves, VCRs or personal computers, all of which seemed intimidating and confusing when you first got them. But would you ever want to do without them now? Once you begin managing your own investments and realizing how easy, how much fun and how profitable it can be, you'll be as happy as I am that you took the initiative.

I truly believe *The 17% Plan* is the most important investment book you could ever read to secure your financial future. After you give it a chance, I'm sure you'll agree.

I'd like to take this opportunity to wish you the best in achieving your financial goals, whatever they may be.

Those who are happy and content are truly wealthy;
How much money it takes, is for each to decide.

Chapter One

Preparing

LOVE THOSE RRSPs

Next to my wife, kids and dog, few things are more dear to me than my Registered Retirement Savings Plan. It enabled me to leave my job and have the lifestyle I wanted when I was 39.

Some of you may not even know what an RRSP actually is, and you may think it's a GIC or something. Quite simply, an RRSP is only an account, or, as the name suggests, a plan. Think of it as a warehouse, but instead of storing furniture, it stores investments. And those investments can be all sorts of things — mutual funds (which obviously I prefer), GICs, stocks, bonds, etc.

The beauty of the RRSP is that it lets money grow in a way that's truly remarkable. This money-making vehicle is such a good one that the name — Registered Retirement Savings — doesn't do it any justice. Those three words conjure up all sorts of negative attitudes, like saving, sacrificing, living in the future, old age, confusion, regulations, etc.

So what tends to happen? We procrastinate, or forget about it, or let someone else take care of it because we don't want the so-called bother. A typical attitude is: "I'll think about it when I'm 65." Many of us spend more time planning a vacation, brushing our teeth or washing our car than we do on our RRSP — if we even have one. Some of us even think RRSPs aren't exciting enough, that they're the poor man's way to invest. As if scotch is better than beer.

If this sounds familiar, don't feel bad. But the point is, you could be settling for far too less financially. It's somewhat ironic that you might be so busy trying to make money at your job that you don't think about how much money you could make with an RRSP.

Some people don't have to work for a living because their money "works" for them. An RRSP, when managed properly, can do an awful lot of work.

For starters, putting money into an RRSP gives you an automatic income tax deduction. For the average person, that means you'll get back about $400 on your income tax return for every $1,000 you put into your plan. In effect, the Government of Canada is helping you with your plan, which is rather nice, don't you think? However, this tax deduction, which is reason enough to contribute to a plan, isn't the main reason to do it.

The real benefit is that the money in the plan grows tax free until you withdraw it, and you'd be amazed at how fast the numbers grow when you earn interest on interest on interest . . .

To understand how money grows, you need to know how many years it takes for money to double. There's an easy way to figure it out. It's called the Rule of 72. Simply take the interest rate and divide it into 72. If, for example, the interest rate was 10 per cent, paid yearly, the money would double every 7.2 years.

Continuing with that 10% rate, and starting with $1,000 in a plan, the money would grow like this:

$1,000	to	$2,000	after	7.2	years;
$2,000	to	$4,000	after	14.4	years;
$4,000	to	$8,000	after	21.6	years;
$8,000	to	$16,000	after	28.8	years;
$16,000	to	$32,000	after	36.0	years;
$32,000	to	$64,000	after	43.2	years;
$64,000	to	$128,000	after	50.4	years.

If you think these figures look good, it gets a lot better. Look what happens when you get a 17% rate of return. Using the Rule of 72, money would double every **4.2** years and the money would grow like this:

$1,000	to	$2,000	after	4.2	years;
$2,000	to	$4,000	after	8.4	years;
$4,000	to	$8,000	after	12.6	years;
$8,000	to	$16,000	after	16.8	years;
$16,000	to	$32,000	after	21.0	years;
$32,000	to	$64,000	after	25.2	years;
$64,000	to	$128,000	after	29.4	years;
$128,000	to	$256,000	after	33.6	years;
$256,000	to	$512,000	after	37.8	years;
$512,000	to	$1,024,000	after	42.0	years;
$1,024,000	to	$2,048,000	after	46.2	years;
$2,048,000	to	$4,096,000	after	50.4	years.

As you can see, a single one-time contribution of $1,000 would grow to over $4 million after 50 years with a 17%

rate of return, compared to only $128,000 with a 10% rate of return.

Now, suppose you put $1,000 PER YEAR into an RRSP, along with the 17% rate of return. You'd end up with $26,000 after 10 years, $152,000 after 20 years, $757,000 after 30 years and, believe it or not, $17 million after 50 years. Imagine the outrageous pile of money you'd have if you contributed $2,000, $3,000, $4,000 or $5,000 a year!

Most of us don't need millions of dollars to live, but I wanted to show you how dramatically money compounds with a higher rate of return. Consider this realistic scenario: If you contribute $3,000 per year, or less than $60 a week, into an RRSP for 20 years, you'll have more than $456,000 if you get a yearly rate of return of 17 per cent. Assuming you continue to earn 17%, you could then take out more than $77,000 from your plan every year, forever. That's my idea of financial freedom.

Oh, by the way, any money withdrawn from an RRSP is taxable, but when you've got almost half a million dollars, it's at least a little easier to swallow.

NOW IS THE TIME

Accumulating money over time is actually quite easy, if you have the will to get started and the discipline to stay with it. Only about one out of four Canadians who are eligible to have an RRSP actually have one, indicating the majority don't even give it a chance.

But hey, visualize getting up in the morning and having the time to enjoy your coffee, rather than drinking it on the run, in a traffic jam and on your way to a job you hate. Imagine, instead, getting into a career you like and having fun. In short, imagine having a choice!

The RRSP gives you a way to accumulate enough money to have that choice; to be able to say goodbye to that wretched boss with bad breath; to be able to stop worrying whether or not you'll be laid off or have enough money to pay your bills; or to be able to just get out of the rat race.

If it feels like you're scurrying around from day to day, barely surviving and with little hope in sight, then it's time to shift your investment program into high gear. It won't solve all of your immediate concerns, but it'll turn on the light at the end of the tunnel and mark the beginning of a new beginning.

There are many excuses for not having a plan. "With inflation, money in an RRSP won't be worth anything anyway," someone once told me. Now that's a real head-scratcher, because it suggests money doesn't help when there's inflation. Excuse me? A more common reason people give for not having a plan is that they don't understand its potential. So, now that you know it, there should be nothing standing in your way — unless, of course, you're a little short of cash.

But in order to have a choice, you have to make a choice. Life is full of tradeoffs, and you may have to give up something to have an RRSP. Setting aside money for a plan is often considered such a sacrifice. However, is it really that bad to spend less in exchange for what you originally thought was only a dream? I sure don't think so.

I know of families that earn $30,000 a year and have an RRSP. I also know of families that make three times that amount but "can't afford" one. When it comes to having, or not having a plan, attitude is frequently the reason, not how much money you make. I worked for a food service company for many years and earned a half-decent wage, but no Brinks truck ever had to pull up to the front door of my house.

Contributing to your plan can be made easy by regularly transferring money from your bank account or pay cheque. Never getting your hands on the money ensures you won't spend it. And you probably won't even miss it. You'll find it becomes as automatic as paying a bill every month.

By making some modest lifestyle choices, you can free up some extra money for your plan. Cutting back on alcohol, restaurants and tobacco might be a good place to start. Go only "half way" around the world on your next vacation. Comparative shop. Look for specials. Buy less-expensive "toys." Become more resourceful and do more of the fixing and repairing yourself. Earn some extra money from your hobbies and things you like doing.

Once you do have an RRSP, congratulate yourself for taking the initiative. It's up to each of us to take care of our futures. Life insurance companies are going under. Career positions are being replaced with service jobs. Job security is now job insecurity. Government pensions — as small as they are — may not be available. Company pensions may not be adequate either, and it makes you wonder how you can contribute to some of these plans for decades, only to receive so little in return. But that's a story for another time. Now's the time to get the most out of your plan.

WAYS TO IMPROVE YOUR RRSP

- Contribute as soon as you can. The earlier the better. The longer money compounds, the harder it "works." Procrastination, therefore, is very expensive.

- Contribute the maximum allowed every year. Yearly limits are 18% of your previous year's earned income to a maximum of $13,500, less a pension adjustment should you belong to a company pension plan. As well, you're allowed to contribute for those previous years where you didn't contribute — back to the 1991 taxation year. Borrow the money if necessary — and if possible — to maximize your contributions. Compounding interest will more than pay for the loan charges, especially when the loan is paid off quickly.

  An often-asked question is: Do you contribute to a plan, or make extra payments against the mortgage? I feel it's a personal decision based on your attitude towards debt. You may feel better lowering your debt level. But when you do some number-crunching, you'll make more money with compounding interest, especially over the longer term. Maximizing your RRSP contributions and then using the tax refund to pay down the mortgage is a good way to go.

- Over-contribute to your plan by up to $8,000. While you won't get an immediate tax break for it, the earnings will be compounding tax-free.

- If you receive a severance package when leaving your employer, put up to $3,500 per year of service directly into your plan. It'll give it a huge boost.

- Also when leaving your employer, consider transferring your company pension plan to your own RRSP. But, before you do, it's vitally important to look at all of the advantages and disadvantages of your company pension. There may be some special rules and benefits to consider.

- Keep the money in your plan as long as possible — that is, until you have enough. Don't take the money out beforehand unless it's a real emergency. Paying tax on the withdrawn money and then forgoing all future compounding interest on that money is the true cost of a withdrawal.

There's a home-buyer plan that allows you, within guidelines, to borrow money from your RRSP for the down payment and then repay it later. Personally, I'd keep my money compounding and try to get the down payment from somewhere else.

- If you're married or live common-law, it's best to have two RRSPs, particularly if one spouse isn't working. A spouse with earned income can contribute to a spousal plan, which then becomes a plan for the other. The advantage of having two plans in two different names is to save on taxes when you withdraw money. By income-splitting, you can save up to 20% in taxes (It's better to have a husband and wife each showing an income of $20,000 a year instead of either one earning all $40,000).

- Increase your rate of return — the ultimate way to improve any investment program, as we showed earlier. How do you get a higher rate of return? Read on.

TAKE CONTROL

Jack D. Schwager, in his *The New Market Wizards*, found that to be a successful investor, you have to have an edge. He wasn't talking about things like insider trading, specialized training or incredibly good luck. Instead, he was talking about being in control.

Control was the driving force behind all of the wizards he interviewed. And not surprisingly, when you look at people who are successful — not just financially — they all tend to have control. They know where they want to go, they set their own course and strive to achieve it. They're often leaders, people you admire and look up to, people you want to associate with.

The way you take control is by developing your own E-D-G-E, through Education, Desire, Goal Setting and Empowerment. And I'd like to briefly talk about these four areas before getting into the nuts and bolts of mutual fund investing and my own strategy.

The EDUCATION required is information — not a financial degree. You can be a successful investor without the letters behind your name. I left university without a degree and I have never found it necessary to go back to learn the technical jargon relating to the investment world. Information lets you make knowledgeable and informed decisions, which more often than not will be the right ones. I'll be showing you what kind of information you'll need, and how to get it, as we go along (There's also an Appendix at the back of the book).

As far as DESIRE, investment management takes some commitment and time, so you have to be willing to put in the effort — definitely more at the beginning if you're just getting your feet wet. Very little worthwhile is ever achieved without effort. If you think there's an easier way, sure, there are plenty of get-rich-quick schemes out there. But most of those schemes make only the promoters rich quick.

Now let's talk about GOAL SETTING. What are your own personal goals, objectives or ambitions? Having a blueprint is a part of any investment program. The goal is wealth creation, so you want to have an idea of how much money you want. Once you decide that, you can figure out how much money you have to contribute and what rate of return on that money is needed.

EMPOWERMENT is confidence. It's believing in yourself and your ability, and having a winning mind-set. You'll find it comes with education and experience.

Taking control of your investment program isn't nearly as hard as you might think. Give yourself time to learn and understand without putting any pressure on yourself. Tell yourself that YOU are the one who is best-suited to manage your investments. After all, who cares more about your money than you do?

Chapter Two

Learning

WHAT TO LOOK FOR IN A MUTUAL FUND

According to one dictionary, a mutual fund is "an investment company that invests its pooled funds in a diversified list of securities." Huh?

Let's make this a little easier. A mutual fund is simply a fund with investments in it. You can buy mutual funds for your RRSP, or you can buy them on their own. Either way, they operate essentially the same.

There are different funds with different investments in them. No two funds are exactly the same. Some funds earn interest, others don't. Some carry more risk than others, have different rules, or do better with particular circumstances.

When you buy a mutual fund, you buy at the fund's current share price, also known as the unit value. Basically, you buy a small piece of all the investments in the fund, and your shares will either rise or fall in value depending on the performance of those investments. Your shares can also make money in a second way — by earning interest, similar to a bank account or a GIC.

Before buying a mutual fund, make sure you know what you're getting into. Like anything else, it's buyer beware. You'd never buy a house without going inside and checking it out. Imagine closing the deal and then finding out the house had no furnace. Surprise! And surprise is what you want to avoid with mutual funds, or any investment for that matter.

The three main things you want to look for are: the risk, the rules, and what's in the fund. Most of that information can be found in the fund's prospectus, which can be intimidating to read. Most of these reports are jammed with figures and financial terms and are so dry you need a glass of water to read them. If there's anything you don't understand, talk to the fund representative. After you've read this book, there shouldn't be much you don't understand.

THE RISKS

The risk with a mutual fund is not with the financial institution selling the fund, but with the investments in it. If an institution were to go bankrupt — and some have — its funds would carry on and be managed by another institution. The Principle Group is one example, and its funds are now managed by Metropolitan Life Insurance Company.

Mutual funds aren't guaranteed investments, and some carry more risk than others and at different times. When the investments in a fund fall in value, so does the share price and, therefore, so does the value of your shares. THAT is the main risk with mutual funds. But there's one exception to this falling share price/losing money equation. It can happen monthly, quarterly or at year-end when a fund pays out interest or distributions. Should the price of the fund go down when the payout occurs, you would wind up with more shares. So you would still have the same amount of money, if not more.

Each mutual fund has a management team, which buys and sells the fund's investments within a set of objectives. The fund manager can be the difference between a high rate of return or a poor one, depending on his or her strategies. Some investors choose funds based solely on the manager, but a word of caution here. Even the best managers can lose their touch or change institutions. If you want to stay with one manager, keep updated on his or her investment objectives and, more importantly, keep abreast of any "address changes."

One way to know how risky a fund is, is to look at its past **yearly** performance. One fund might earn 15% one year and 15% the next, which is more stable than a fund earning 30% one year and nothing the next. Financial institutions often give the one-, three- and five-year rates of returns. If you notice the one-year return is very high and the five-year rate is a lot lower, then the fund has performed poorly or even had losses in the middle years. Some mutual fund prices can fluctuate wildly throughout the year and then end up little changed. This can give the illusion that a fund is fairly steady when it's not.

Financial institutions often use a volatility chart to describe which funds are riskier than others. These charts may be helpful over a number of years, but they can be misleading. Some funds that normally carry less risk are quite risky at times. Mortgage and bond funds, for example, are supposed to be two of the safer funds, but they're not when interest rates are low and then starting to rise.

When discussing and analyzing risk, your own personal views and tolerances are indeed your own. The only thing I might say is that as you get older, you normally want less risk because you have less time to recoup any losses. That aside, there's always some risk when you try to earn a higher rate of return, and the mere mention of the word *risk* sends out the red flags and keeps some investors in guaranteed investments like term deposits and GICs. But those can be costly if they're holding down your rate of return. Remember the Rule of 72, and how money compounds?

The real issue with investing isn't about buying guaranteed or non-guaranteed investments. It's not even about earning the highest possible rate of return, per se. It's about earning the best rate of return WITHIN YOUR TOLERANCE FOR RISK. Mutual funds may not be guaranteed investments as such, but once you better understand them, you'll find they do let you invest comfortably and successfully. Until 1987, when I began investing in mutual funds, I used to be a GIC man myself. Frankly, I can no longer afford the guarantee.

THE RULES

A little earlier, we talked about avoiding surprises. Remember the house with no furnace? With a mutual fund, you want to have a good look at the foundation and there are three major things to check out:

- WHEN can you buy or sell shares of the fund?
- HOW do you do it?
- WHAT are the fees or charges?

You can buy or sell mutual funds only on what's called Valuation Day, when the share prices are calculated. Find out if the funds are valued daily, weekly, monthly or whenever, and if there is anything special. With some funds, you have to stay in them for a period of time, or, if you sell them, you can't get back in for a while. And sometimes you have to buy or sell before a specific time. Personally, I like the freedom of being able to buy or sell, or to switch funds, on any business day.

How you buy or sell the funds is another question you want answered. What steps do you have to go through? Can you do it by phone? Do you have to sign papers? Do you need a broker or advisor, and, if so, is he or she accessible? You should also receive confirming statements or receipts every time you buy or sell.

There are management fees associated with all mutual funds. These fees are not paid for up front. They come out of the fund itself and more or less lower the fund's overall rate of return. They're approximately 2% or 3% per year, which is no big deal if the fund is making money. Don't worry about pennies when there are dollars involved.

Mutual funds may also have sales charges, brokerage fees and/or redemption costs. These can wind up being significant, especially if you have to pay up front. The charges, known as load fees, are over and above the normal management fees. You'll find differing opinions as to the benefits of load funds versus non-load funds. My own opinion is that load fees are worth it, but only if you receive good value in return, such as sound financial advice or a mutual fund you're happy with.

You should question paying load fees if you're not getting your money's worth. If all things are equal, why pay to invest? You may as well have ALL of your money working for YOU, not somebody else. It bugs me to see companies trying to recruit mutual fund sales people by telling them they can make huge commissions.

You may not realize you can buy or sell mutual funds yourself. It's as easy as going to the corner store. You can simply visit or phone any number of institutions and they'll be glad to serve you. You may still have to pay load fees for certain funds, but those fees are often lower if you eliminate the middle man. In other words, you can negotiate.

Don't think that a fund will perform better if you pay more to invest in it. There's no connection between load fees and how well a fund performs. Performance is related to the investments, not the fees. Recent surveys show that no-load funds are every bit as good as comparable load funds.

I prefer no-load funds because they're less costly and I don't want to let costs stand in the way of my decisions. If you hang on to a losing fund to avoid paying a redemption fee, you may as well hang up on a higher rate of return. Click.

WHAT'S IN THE FUND

The name of the fund will give you an idea of which investments are in the fund. Most mutual funds will fit into one of the following types:

- Treasury bill funds
- Mortgage funds
- Bond funds
- Equity funds
- Specialty funds
- Foreign funds
- Dividend funds
- Balanced funds

TREASURY BILL funds, also known as money market funds, contain Government of Canada treasury bills (T-Bills). These funds are the closest thing you'll find to a GIC. They earn interest from the T-Bills based on current interest rates. One important thing about most of these funds is that the share price remains constant. However, the amount of interest they earn will fluctuate just like a GIC. What's the risk with these funds? It's really whether or not our government is going to pay the interest . . . don't laugh, stranger things have happened. But it is rather remote.

MORTGAGE funds invest primarily in residential first mortgages. They earn interest from the mortgages, and their share prices fluctuate with current mortgage rates. The main thing to remember is this: When mortgage rates fall, mortgage fund share prices rise; when mortgage rates rise, mortgage fund shares prices fall.

The reason can be a little confusing, but if you really want to know, here's why: When mortgage rates fall, the mortgages already in the fund are then worth more (and vice-versa). Think of it this way: When interest rates fall, an original GIC still paying 10% would be worth more than the new one now paying 9%.

BOND funds contain Government of Canada, Provincial and Corporate bonds. These are different than your regular Canada Saving Bonds. They earn interest the same way, but their value fluctuates with the bond market. Therefore, when the bond market rises, bond fund share prices rise.

The bond market generally rises with falling interest rates (and vice-versa). When interest rates fall, previously issued bonds with higher rates are then worth more, which raises prices.

EQUITY OR GROWTH funds invest in, and fluctuate with, the stock market. They may earn interest (called dividends), but normally less than T-Bill, Mortgage and Bond funds. Just a thought here: Don't buy equity funds for the dividends. The dividends are peanuts compared to the usual fluctuations in the share price.

SPECIALTY funds are equity type funds, but the investments in these funds are concentrated in specific areas. Precious metal funds, for example, invest mostly in gold and gold shares. Other specialty funds include real estate funds, resource funds and small company (small cap) funds. Speciality funds don't earn interest, and the share prices tend to fluctuate more than the other funds. When any equity type funds are smaller in dollar value (say, $10 million or less), have fewer investments in them or are less diversified, their share prices tend to fluctuate more.

FOREIGN or International funds are those which invest outside of Canada. They contain stocks, bonds or other investments. Their share prices move with the foreign markets AND with exchange rates. The currency factor comes into play with most foreign funds. Assuming all else is constant, WHEN THE CANADIAN DOLLAR FALLS, FOREIGN MUTUAL FUND SHARE PRICES RISE.

That's not a misprint. I've met investors who believe it's the other way around. A full explanation can get rather technical, so to make a long story short, a rising foreign currency will buy more Canadian dollars. And more Canadian dollars makes the fund worth more.

The currency factor has a large influence on a fund's share price. The reason for buying foreign funds is often for the currency play rather than for the actual stocks or bonds in them. Again assuming all else is constant, if the Canadian dollar falls by 1%, then the foreign fund will rise by 1%. Some foreign funds do not have the currency factor.

DIVIDEND funds are, as the name suggests, dividend-oriented. They invest primarily in higher-quality stocks which pay higher interest, but their share prices also fluctuate with the stock market.

BALANCED funds are just that — balanced. These funds, also known as growth and income funds, generally invest in a wider range of investments and are more or less a combination of the other seven funds. They're the smorgasbord fund instead of the single entrée, and some portions can be larger than others.

One final, important thought before leaving this section. I said earlier that the name of the fund gives you an idea of what's in the fund. But the name doesn't tell you everything, so take the extra step and find out EXACTLY what's in the fund.

My younger brother Terry once bought a mortgage fund, thinking it consisted only of mortgages. He noticed that the share price kept inching down and he couldn't figure it out. So he called the institution. It was only then that he discovered the mortgage fund also had a large percentage of bonds in it. And guess what . . . the bond market had been falling, dragging the mortgage fund down with it. Surprise!

Terry was a little cheesed off, but moreso at himself after I politely suggested it was his responsibility to find out what was in the fund beforehand.

HOW TO CHOOSE A MUTUAL FUND

LEARN the fund's ground rules:
- when the fund is valued.
- how you buy or sell.
- what the load fees are (if there are any).
- if there is anything special about the fund.

WEIGH the fund's risk by looking at:
- its past yearly performance.
- how volatile its share price is.
- its size and number of years in operation.

CONFIRM what's in the fund, and how much interest, if any, it will earn.

DETERMINE what moves the fund's share price:
- mortgage rates.
- the bond market.
- the stock market.
- international bond or stock markets.
- currency values.
- precious metal prices.

DECIDE:
- if you are comfortable with the fund's rules and risks.
- if you are satisfied with the income you will receive.
- if the relevant financial market(s) are likely to rise or fall.

PROVEN PRINCIPLES

Earning a higher rate of return takes more than simply choosing a mutual fund, unless by chance you happen to choose a top performer. And even if do you, there's no guarantee it'll continue to shine in the future. In fact, choosing the best past-performers is often a poor strategy because it's common for funds that are stellar performers one year to be dogs the next.

Making decisions based solely on what has happened is a trap many investors fall into. The statement "Past performance is not a guarantee of future results," is inserted into most mutual fund advertising. Now, if that's not a clue to look beyond the past and into the future, I don't know what is.

Your rate of return with a mutual fund — or any investment — hinges on how it performs AFTER you buy it. It's easy to get caught up in the current news and advertising, but you have to base your decisions on what you think will occur in the future. Predicting the direction of the financial markets is a billion-dollar industry. The explanations and reasons are endless. Some are logical, others aren't.

You can ask the professionals for help on future direction, but they often only agree to disagree. It's a little amusing when five different analysts or economists are asked the same question and two say one thing, two say another and the last one sits on the fence. As the saying goes: If all the economists in the world were laid end to end, they still wouldn't reach a conclusion. So, if **they** can't agree, and if **they** are often wrong, then what are **we** supposed to do?

We stay diversified! Remember that old saying, "Never put all your eggs in one basket?" The home-run hitter strikes out more often than other players. Similarly, if you put all of your capital into a single investment, trying for the huge gains, you, too, run a greater risk of going down swinging. Hitting the doubles and triples will still produce a good batting average.

When you diversify, you don't want to lose on any part of your portfolio. But you often do if you over-diversify because cancelling-out tends to occur. Not all of the funds make money at the same time, so you have to be selective. If you went to a horse race, for example, you wouldn't bet on all eight horses — unless you wanted three winners and five losers. I'm no expert on the nags, but I don't think you can make money that way.

What you do **after** you choose your funds is just as critical as picking them. A wise investor never buys and then forgets, because things change. Financial markets rise and fall; interest and inflation rates change directions; the economy is alternately strong and weak; the Canadian dollar fluctuates; governments change; emotions change; fear or greed can set in, distorting supply and demand. I'm not saying you have to be on top of everything all the time, but the point is, you do have to keep an eye on your funds.

Change can happen quickly — sometimes right after you buy a fund — or it can happen over a period of time. I know of funds that earned more than 100% one year, only to lose almost 50% the next. None of us wants that kind of a bombshell, but it can happen if you buy funds at the wrong time and then forget about them. We should all be like elephants, because you know what they say about elephants . . . (If you don't know, see Appendix, Page 80).

The best way to know how a fund is performing is to follow the share price. Unfortunately, you'll pick the odd dog. Everyone does. But when it happens, dump it to avoid any more losses. Preserving capital is absolutely essential because once it's gone, your investing days are over. So take a small loss before it becomes a big one. If you've diversified properly, the gains in your other funds should offset any of those minor losses.

Another reason to monitor your funds is to keep your capital working hard all the time. When something changes to make one fund more attractive than another, why not move some of your capital into it?

Consider the following list, which shows the average 10-year rates of returns of the different mutual funds to June 30, 1994:

T-Bill funds	8.4%
mortgage funds	10.1%
bond funds	11.1%
Canadian stock funds	9.7%
international stock funds	13.3%
specialty funds	7.1%
dividend funds	8.9%
balanced funds	9.8%

Clearly, you are **not** going to get a 17% rate of return over the long term by buying and holding the average mutual fund. The way you get it is by moving your money around, and we'll show you how in the next chapter. The Canadian Financial Market Report on the following page shows how the markets fluctuate. You can see the benefits of investing in specific markets at specific times.

The Canadian Financial Market Report (Yearly percentage rates of return)			
Year	**Canadian Stocks**	**Canadian Bonds**	**T-Bills**
1980	30.1	6.6	15.0
1981	-10.2	4.2	18.4
1982	5.5	35.4	15.4
1983	35.5	11.5	9.6
1984	-2.4	14.7	11.6
1985	25.1	21.2	9.9
1986	9.0	14.7	9.3
1987	5.9	4.0	8.5
1988	11.1	9.8	9.4
1989	21.4	12.8	12.4
1990	-14.8	7.6	13.5
1991	12.0	22.1	9.8
1992	-1.4	9.8	7.1
1993	32.6	18.1	5.5

Note:
Not all mutual funds reflect the market figures. Some had much greater percentage increases or decreases during these years or specific time frames.

I once attended a seminar where a mutual fund salesman was full of excitement explaining the virtues of equity investing. He was saying that all you had to do to earn 15% to 25% per year on your money was invest in this one particular fund every month. The fund happened to have a 10-year rate of return of less than 9%. Taking his commission into account, the rate of return would have been even lower.

The real truth with mutual funds is that it's rare for any fund to consistently earn 15 to 25%. You'll see for yourself by looking at the monthly reports that are available. THESE REPORTS ARE EXCELLENT! They give you the facts, like the average rates of return you saw on Page 31. They're also good if you want to see how your fund stacks up against the others. The Globe and Mail, The Financial Times and The Calgary Herald, to name a few, all print monthly mutual fund reports.

I don't disagree with the typical buy-and-hold investment strategy if that suits you. But buying a fund "for the long term" suggests you stay with it even when it goes down. Does that mean you should be intent on earning a low rate of return — or even losing money — for several years even when there are alternatives? Frankly, if you buy into a fund at the wrong time and stay with it, it may take "a long term" to get your capital back. Gold is currently around $400 an ounce. Remember when it was $860 (U.S.) in 1979?

I certainly hope you don't hang on to losing funds out of loyalty to either the fund or whoever sold it to you. Some people think that when a fund goes down, it's only a paper loss, but the bottom line is that your investment is worth less. If you had a flat tire, you'd fix it. So keep your mutual funds motoring along, too.

Change of any sort scares many people. But it can also be a good thing. When change negatively affects one type of fund, it can benefit another. Frequently, the more the markets change, the greater the opportunity. The more they fall, the higher they can rise.

THE FALLACY OF DOLLAR-COST AVERAGING

Dollar-cost averaging is systematically contributing (i.e. every month or so) to a mutual fund. The theory is that you get more bang for your buck because you catch the dips in the market. Sure you do, but what about your money that's been in the fund all along? I think it's great to systematically contribute to an investment program, but you still want all of your money working as hard as possible all the time. Too often that doesn't happen, and that's just one of the reasons why I disagree with dollar-cost averaging. The others are:

1. Dollar-cost averaging assumes the share price will rise after it falls. Even if it does, you don't know when. And what if the price is still low when you want to sell your shares?

2. A mutual fund's share price can move in different directions other than falling first and then rising. Contributing to a fund with a share price that rises first and then falls will result in losses if you buy in near the top.

3. Dollar-cost averaging is often done with only one equity fund, which I believe is not a diversified enough approach. Assume you have $50,000 in one fund and over the following year that fund falls in value by 20%. Now you would have only $40,000 — not including any monthly contributions. That's hardly a way to preserve capital.

4. The average mutual fund rate of return over the last 10 years is approximately 10%. Dollar-cost averaging with these funds will **not** get you a substantially higher rate of return. Buying more shares when the markets are low, and buying less when the markets are high, largely cancels itself out.

5. The following graphs show how much better it is to move your money around successfully. Never think it's advantageous for the fund's share price to fall when you're in that fund. Working the numbers proves the point vividly:

The "V"

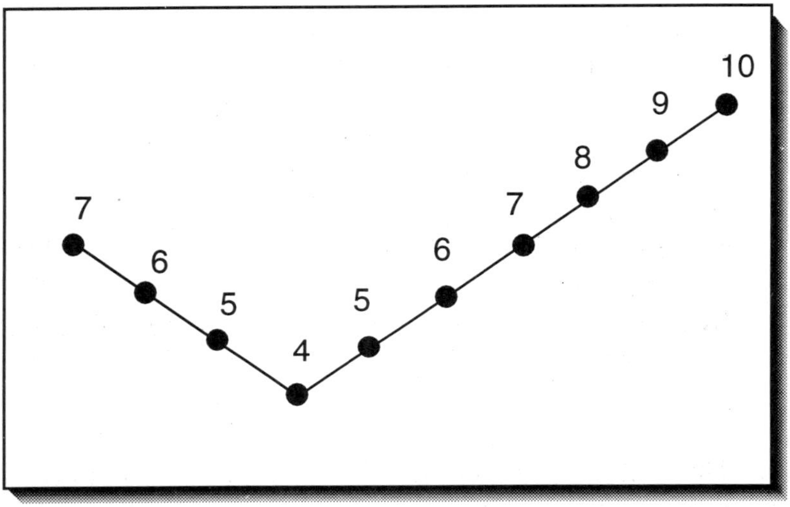

- the share price starts at $7, falls to $4 and then rises to $10.

- $50,000 was invested at the starting share price and another $1,000 per year, over 10 years, was put into the fund at each dollar value.

total shares purchased	=	8,748.03
final share price	=	$10.00
total value	=	**$87,480.30**

The Hill

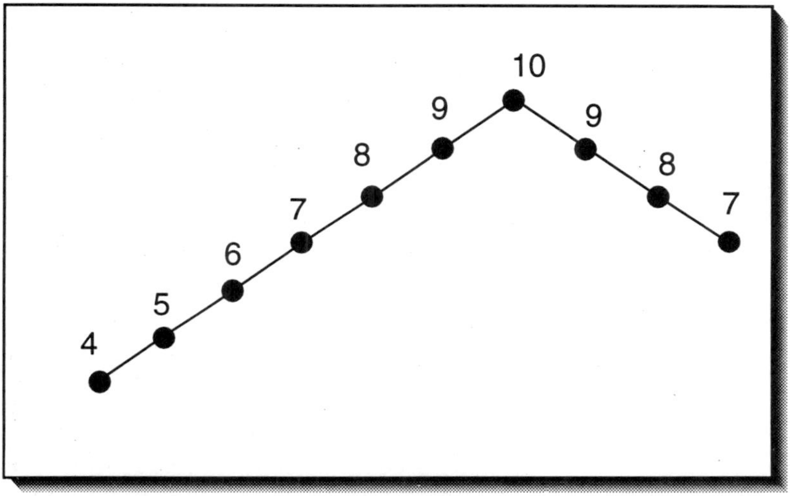

- the share price starts at $4, rises to $10 and then falls back to $7.

- $50,000 was invested at the starting share price and another $1,000 per year, over 10 years, was put into the fund at each dollar value.

total shares purchased	=	13,974.61
final share price	=	$7.00
total value	=	**$97,822.27**

The Straight Line

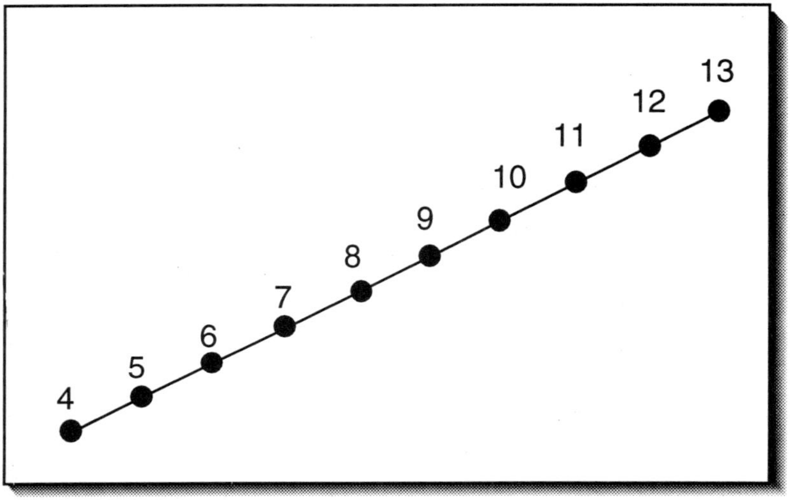

- the share price starts at $4 and rises steadily to $13.

- $50,000 was invested at the starting share price and another $1,000 per year, over 10 years, was put into the fund at each dollar value.

total shares purchased	=	13,846.80
final share price	=	$13.00
total value	=	**$180,008.40**

Clearly, when you compare $180,008 to $97,822 and $87,480, dollar-cost averaging with falling share prices will cost you a lot of money. Move your capital around to go for the straight line.

CHECKLIST FOR SUCCESSFUL INVESTING

1. Know yourself and your tolerance for risk.

2. Avoid emotion. Investing is strictly business.

3. Simplify. Set guidelines. Develop a system that suits you.

4. Do business with reputable companies and agents. Justify all costs that reduce profit.

5. Buy only investments you fully understand.

6. Base decisions on what you believe will happen in the future. Past performance is in the past.

7. Preserve capital. Stay diversified.

8. Monitor your investments. Watch for change.

9. Change your investments to keep profits and prevent large losses. Look for greater opportunity.

10. Learn from your successes and failures. Maintain records. Always know where your money is and how it's performing.

WHY I LOVE MUTUAL FUNDS

Mutual Funds give me a way to invest;
With the control, for a good night's rest.

I can pick and choose the funds I desire;
Easily and quickly and when I require.

Simple to understand, and follow I tell;
And not only that, inexpensive as well.

A higher rate of return is the quest;
Mutual Funds have passed **my** *test.*

There is overall less risk with mutual funds. Owning a piece of 100 companies, for example, is safer than investing in only one. By diversifying with different types of funds, the risk is reduced even further.

Professional management also helps to reduce risk. Money managers use their expertise to buy, sell and manage the individual investments in the fund. All I do is decide which funds will perform the best and when.

Mutual funds hold investments from all over the world — investments that I couldn't buy on my own. More choice brings more opportunity.

With mutual funds you have control, and to me, that's the EDGE. They are easy to monitor, primarily by watching the funds' share prices in the newspaper, or by calling the financial institution. Buying or selling shares is based on the value of the fund, so, unlike the open markets, you don't have to worry about finding sellers or buyers when you want to make a move. You can also make your move quickly, just about on demand, cost-free and easily, simply by making a phone call or signing a piece of paper.

WOW! I have yet to see any other investment that gives you CONTROL, CHOICE, POTENTIAL, LESS RISK and LOW COSTS all at once.

The purpose for investing in mutual funds is to earn a rate of return that is higher than a guaranteed investment. Otherwise, there wouldn't be much point. Beating GIC rates without enduring a high level of risk is my idea of winning. I've been able to do it, which is why I love mutual funds. You don't even have to choose the best-performing funds, and you can even make some wrong choices and still be a winner. If I can do it, so can you. It's time to show you how.

Chapter Three

Winning

THE YO YOs

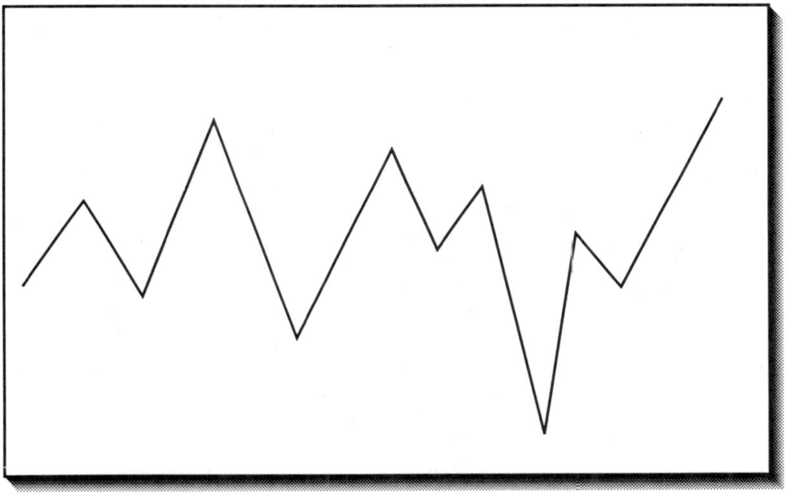

The financial markets and the factors that affect them move up and down much like a yo yo. Economic cycles, interest rates, currencies, commodity prices, etc., all rise and fall, only to rise and fall again. What remains then, is a continual pattern, in which you can conclude that a low price or number is more likely to rise, while a high one is more apt to fall. Playing the yo-yo action is the essence to winning and actually beating the markets, but not in the conventional sense.

The phrase "Buy low and sell high" really means nothing to me. What is high and what is low? Prices are up and down all the time. The graph on the previous page could be drawn every day, week, month or year. Trying to base decisions on the absolute highs and lows is too restrictive and a pretty good way to get stressed out.

There's only one low and one high, with all sorts of larger and smaller gyrations in between. It would be great to be able to predict them, but, of course, we can't. To complicate matters, prices never move in straight lines. They trend. Prices that are trending up will fall occasionally along the way, while prices that are trending down will rise every so often. It may also be hard to know at times when prices are "treading water" or actually starting to change direction.

You've probably heard all of the endless reasons why markets rise and fall — from the state of the economy to technical factors to market sentiment. But the truth of the matter is that there's sometimes no apparent reason for why things happen. Market watchers often debate whether we're in a bull or bear market . . . Or whether we're in a correction in a bull market or at the start of a bear market . . . Or whatever.

I really don't care what it's called because prices rise and fall within bull and bear markets alike, and YOU CAN MAKE MONEY IN EITHER MARKET! You can sometimes lose focus when trying to label a market or look too much at the "big picture." The bottom line is that prices continually rise and fall and **that** is what to consider with any investing system.

Market prices tend to discount the current news and fluctuate with differing expectations of economic and monetary trends six to nine months into the future. Mix into that any current uncertainty, surprise or emotion, and you have the basis for continually rising and falling prices.

The markets can make you look either very good or very bad, and they can do it quickly. Just when you think you've got them all figured out, something changes to wipe out your theories.

Therefore, you need to have a plan which takes market fluctuations into account and also capitalizes on them. Mutual fund share prices, for the most part, mirror the markets they are investing in. Winning with mutual funds is knowing **when** to buy and sell the different funds, which I talk about next.

INTEREST RATES: THE MARKET-MOVER

If there's one factor that moves the financial markets the most, it's got to be changing interest rates. It's the "Mother" of all market movers. Economies revolve around the cost of money. It impacts the levels of government spending, the profitability of companies that borrow money, cash flows and consumer spending power.

About fluctuating interest rates:

a) When rates are high and falling, bond and mortgage funds tend to be the best performers.

b) When rates are lower and fairly stable or continuing to fall, equity funds are often the best place to be.

c) When rates are rising, or expected to rise, it's time to invest mostly in Treasury Bill funds.

Mortgage funds and bond funds perform their absolute best when interest rates are high and falling. The mortgages and bonds pay more interest and the share prices normally rise. Conversely, when interest rates are low and rising, mortgage and bond funds perform poorly. The falling share prices will more than cancel out the interest you receive.

Generally, rising interest rates create doom and gloom. I'll always remember the October stock market crash of 1987, which, not coincidently, came after interest rates rose by close to 40% since the beginning of that year. While there are times a specific fund may do fine despite rising rates, for the most part, save yourself some grief and stay out of the markets when the rates are rising. Don't be afraid to park a large portion of your capital in a treasury bill fund. Sometimes the best-performing fund is one that earns very little, while the other ones are losing.

The Government of Canada sets the interest rate every Tuesday by adding 25 cents to the interest rate of the 90-day treasury bill. Knowing that, you can follow the movement of the rates on a weekly basis.

The government takes various factors into consideration when setting the rates, but inflation is the main one. The markets don't like inflation, except, perhaps, for gold.

To get an idea of where interest rates are headed, first see where the "yo yo" is. When interest rates are near extreme ends, it's only reasonable that they'll start to reverse themselves. Falling bond market prices are also a prelude to rising interest rates. This indicates that the big-boy investors believe interest rates are going up, and following their lead is often good enough for me.

I like to watch the United States bond market for clues to where Canadian interest rates are headed. When the U.S. 30-year Treasury Bond is trending down, rising interest rates are often close behind. When the U.S. Federal Reserve speaks, everyone around the world listens and talks about it.

Critics suggest you can't predict interest-rate direction with any degree of certainty. That's not necessarily so. I like to compare it to a tornado on the horizon. You can see the funnel clouds and black skies, and you can feel the wind as it swirls around menacingly. As the storm approaches, you close up shop and head for the safety of the basement. Even if the tornado doesn't hit, at least you've protected yourself.

Similarly, you get out of the markets if the interest-rate cloud starts to form. Even if the rates don't go higher after you've pulled out, and even if the markets continue to climb, you'll still be earning some money in a T-Bill fund.

But, there **are** indeed times when it's virtually guaranteed that the storm will hit. On Friday, February 4, 1994, Alan Greenspan, the fellow in charge of setting interest rates in the United States, announced a rate increase after several years of declines. This was also at a time when interest rates were at all-time lows. Did this represent a changing trend? You bet! The writing was on the wall, even though many "experts" were saying not to worry. Mortgage and bond funds, and to a lesser extent stock funds, took a pounding over the following months. Investors who originally thought bond and mortgage funds were lower risk, thought differently after losing up to 15 per cent in six months.

And so, on February 4 of 1994, knowing that the bond and stock markets were near all-time highs, that interest rates were at historic lows and rising, and that rising interest rates are bad news, informed investors starting selling that very day. The yo yo was on its way down.

Following interest rates gives you an insight on the future direction of various markets. Even if you don't want to watch them that closely, you will still protect your capital and make money by using the TWO FUNDAMENTAL RULES OF WINNING.

WINNING RULE #1: BUY LOWER

It's a simple rule, yet many investors are inclined to do the opposite!

"The herd is running the fastest, just before it falls over the cliff," is such a suitable expression. After big gains have been made and when prices are high is the time many emotional investors buy, regardless of how many times they've been advised not to. It may seem like the right time to buy, but it's not. Remember the yo yo? It's more likely for share prices to fall after gains, so you should be buying after declines.

The only test that remains, then, is to determine when the loss is big enough, or in other words, when is lower? Share prices can go back up after a drop of one per cent, or they can fall 30 per cent before recovering. Lower could be both the 1% and the 30% drops. The fact is, you can't establish a lower point until the price turns around. THAT IS LOWER.

Now, buying lower doesn't automatically mean it will be the right time to buy, because prices can recover and then start to fall again. It just means it's a better time to buy because prices that are lower are more likely to rise than fall.

The Backward Check

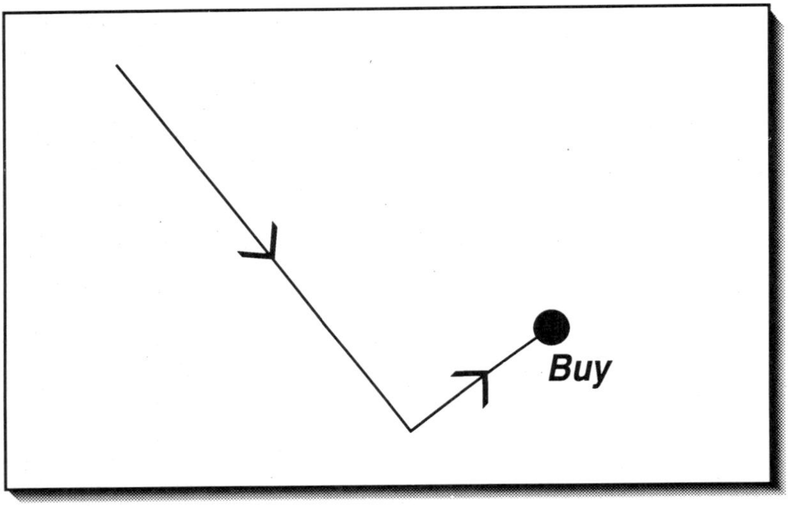

A mutual fund that has fallen and is now starting to rise again would look like a backward check on a graph. These trends can be short term or long term. The declines can be relatively minor or steep. The more severe the decline before the recovery, the greater the potential for the gains to continue.

By looking for the lower prices, you'll often be going against the norm. People thought I was off my rocker when I said the stock market crash of 1987 would eventually turn out to be good news (I took some small losses and sold all of my equity funds the week prior to the crash). Over the following two years, the stock market went up almost 40 per cent. I also recommended the overall stock market at the beginning of 1993 when many articles were saying it was "the year to be cautious." It turned out to be a banner year.

I don't consider myself to be a master market-timer who can predict all of the ups and downs. I'm more of a fundamentalist, and when I say a particular market is the place to invest, it's mainly because the numbers are lower and rising.

Mutual fund advertising is more prevalent after rates of return over a particular time frame are high. You won't see much advertising when performances are miserable. That's the nature of the beast as all companies — financial or otherwise — will attempt to put their best foot forward. But the advertising can make a fund appear to be less risky or better than it actually is. It attracts investors to buy when it's often the wrong time, when prices are high. Then, when they go down and investors start losing money, mutual funds are said to be "long-term investments." Does this sound familiar?

Frankly, when I see funds advertising high rates of return, I remind myself of the herd mentality and run the **other** way. That isn't to say the funds won't continue to perform well, because some will. But it's just more likely they won't.

With any buy system, you also need a sell system . . .

WINNING RULE #2: USE A 5% (OR LESS) CUT-LOSS

In this business, it's not what you make but rather what you keep. An investment has to be sold before all of the profits have been lost. If you do well one year, only to lose it all the next, it's certainly counter-productive. But it's even worse to stay with a fund that starts to rack up heavy losses.

A cut-loss puts an easy procedure in place that tells you when to sell. It removes most of the emotion, secures profits and sets a limit on losses. THERE IS NEVER A REASON TO TAKE LARGE LOSSES, or get caught in a major market correction (a fancy term for losing money), even if you buy in at the worst possible time.

With a 5% cut-loss, the time to sell is **whenever** the mutual fund share price falls by 5% (unless the fall is due to distribution payouts). This rule restricts your losses to no more than 5% — unless the markets take a rare, very large, one-day drop — and it also keeps any profits over 5%. Suppose, for example, you buy $10 shares, which then rise to $12 and start to fall. The sell signal is a fall of 5% from $12, which is $11.40 (95% x $12), ensuring a profit of $1.40 or 14% ($1.40 divided by $10 x 100).

Never buck a trend. Use the cut-loss and get out of funds that may be affected by market corrections. It's true there is a fund manager looking after the investments, but he or she can only limit the losses, not prevent them. During a market correction, it's not uncommon for mutual fund investors to redeem or sell their shares. If enough do, the fund managers may have to sell some of the investments in the funds to generate enough cash to cover the redemptions. This will put even more downward pressure on the markets, causing the prices to fall even more. The more the prices fall, the more other investors may start to sell, which can produce a downward spiral.

What happens much more often, though, are the small, agonizing, continual losses that add up. When the markets fall 5%, then it's believed they'll bounce right back. After they fall another 5%, it's viewed as a buying opportunity. After they fall another 5%, shoulders are shrugged and it's felt that you might as well now stay put. Then when they fall again, the "that's enough of that" emotion sets in — along with the sell order. This is normally the time you want to be smiling and buying lower instead, and the cut-loss will put you in a position to do just that.

Averaging down is a form of dollar-cost averaging, but on a more short-term basis. Basically, it is putting more capital into a fund after the share price has fallen in order to lower your overall share cost. While I may take some heat for this from the more sophisticated investors, DO NOT AVERAGE DOWN! Throwing good money after bad, breaks all of the rules of investing wisely. By putting more money into the fund, you must be now less diversified. Should the share price continue to fall, larger and deeper losses will be incurred.

Sure, averaging down can work at times. And sure, it's possible for a fund's share price to start rising right after you sold with the cut-loss. Even so, my advice is to remain steadfast with the cut-loss rule. My reasons:

1. Preserving capital is more important than earning.

2. Locking in smaller profits, which **may** cause you to miss larger ones, is better than losing all of the profits.

3. You can always buy back into that same fund later.

4. You can pick another fund that performs just as well anyway.

5. It makes decision-making emotion free.

THE WINNING STRATEGY

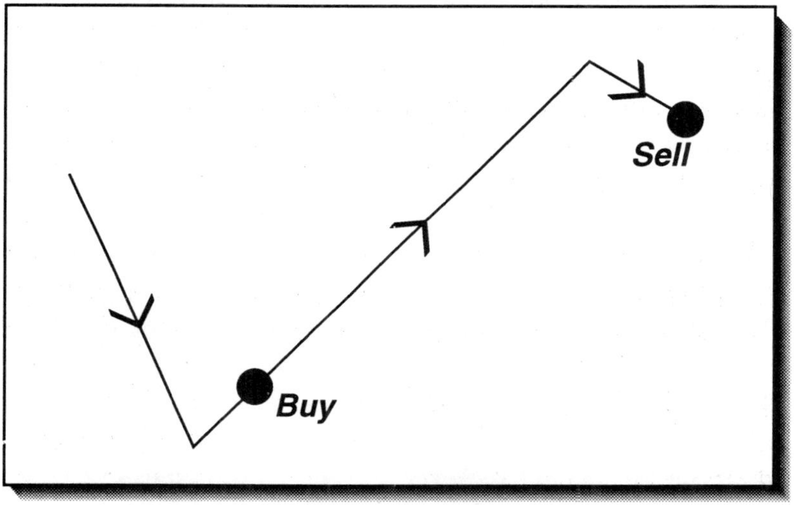

Buying a mutual fund after its share price has recovered, and then selling after it has started to fall, is the buy-lower, sell-higher strategy of successful investing. What you are doing is making money on the spread. Buying on the way down is too risky because you never know how far the price will fall, or when it will start to rise again. Conversely, a fund that is falling after having peaked, signals that the trend is now changing to the down side.

What triggers you to buy are the parameters that suggest there's been a change of direction. It could be improving economic trends, inflation or interest rates that are no longer rising, or starting to fall. It could be government policy that would benefit a particular fund, or a changing direction for currency or commodity prices that would also benefit a certain fund. However, the numbers will generally speak for themselves.

The absolute best time to buy is **after** a market correction or after a fund has been dogging it for some time. Eventually the prices turn around, and when they do, IT'S PROFIT TIME. Bond funds in 1981 performed terribly, but in 1982 they were fantastic performers. Stock funds after the Crash of 87 earned an average of almost 40% over the following two years. Japanese funds started to soar in February of 1993 after years of losses. These are perhaps extreme examples, but there are lots of good buying opportunities happening just about all of the time, all over the world.

A 5% cut-loss takes into account how markets fluctuate in the short term without changing longer-term direction. After a 2% drop in the share price, it's just as likely for the price to go back up again, especially if it's still relatively low. You don't want to sell after only a tiny drop because the price could then take off again.

Refer to the graph at the beginning of this chapter and imagine how well you could do if you continually bought at the lower points and sold at the higher ones. THAT'S HOW YOU GET A HIGHER RATE OF RETURN! The only commitment this strategy requires is to simply watch the share prices so you know when they are lower or higher. Sound simple? It is! Investing successfully doesn't take years of study, volumes of information, baffling criteria and complicated procedures.

It's not necessary to wait for your cut-loss rule before selling, if every indication suggests that a downward trend has started or is about to start. You may also want to have a smaller cut-loss for the less-volatile funds.

Any strategy you use will occasionally fail, and the buy-lower, sell-higher strategy is no exception. It's possible to buy into a fund after it has recovered, only for it to start to fall again. Don't be dismayed by the occasional loss. Your other gains should far outweigh them. And remember, even the funds you may have previously lost on will eventually have their day. There's an element of satisfaction when you buy back into those funds at an even lower price and then watch them soar.

The last thing I'd like to talk about in this section is market psychology — or perhaps, reverse psychology. Prices often rise when you'd just about swear they should go down. So often, when there's high unemployment, layoffs, poor profits, worry, frustration and negativity, the markets rise. Bad news, then, is typically good news for the markets for two main reasons: there's less chance for undesirables like inflation and high interest rates; and nothing lasts forever, which means bad news always gives way to brighter days. On the other hand, lots of optimism usually triggers falling prices. Too much good news brings on bad news, regularly starting with rising inflation and interest rates.

To sum up, you can try to analyze the markets all you want, but the only thing you can really go by is the numbers, so forget all the noise. The numbers are cold, factual and unemotional, so let them tell you when it's time to buy or sell.

THE 17% PLAN

My mutual fund investing, which is done within my RRSP, is based on the principles discussed in this book, using the KISS approach — **K**eep **I**t **S**imple **S**illy.

Highlights:

- I use only one institution, with a branch close to where I live. The bank has a 1-800 number for customer service and current mutual fund share prices.

- The institution manages more than 15 funds, some of them world-wide. They have average track records, and these are the only funds I invest in.

- The funds value daily.

- There are no charges of any kind except normal management fees.

- Confirming statements are received within a week, every time a transaction is made. Quarterly summary statements are also received.

- I spend about 10 minutes a day on my plan.

I can buy, sell or switch funds any business day to take profits, cut losses or take advantage of opportunities, all cost-free. Switching funds is instantaneous. Only a phone call and follow-up signature are required. There are no delays, no restrictions, no confusion and no hassles (And no tax considerations because it's all done within an RRSP). TRULY INVESTING MADE EASY!

By investing in only one company's funds, I reduce time, costs and complications. I've got less paperwork and research, and I can monitor the funds easier. It also eliminates the need to go through a brokerage firm and use a self-directed RRSP.

In a self-directed RRSP, you have access to a variety of different companies and investments. I personally find them more time-consuming, and more difficult and costly to manage. I've got enough potential with my institution's 15 funds that are continually fluctuating. While other companies may have better-performing funds at times, it seems that over the longer term, most funds tend to reflect the market averages anyway.

The institution I use is not unique. Many offer the same service and benefits. It's how you invest in the funds that makes the difference! Every day, I RECORD THE

MUTUAL FUND SHARE PRICES (Sample form at the end of this section). It's an easy way to monitor the funds and the markets. It shows you when a particular fund is either rising or falling.

My approach:

I watch for the funds that have taken a beating, dropping at least 10% from their high. When I see one, I wait for it to recover about 3% from its low. That's a definite buy signal. The numbers suggest an upward price trend in its EARLY stages. A 3% rise tells me it's not just a short-term blip, but that other investors are jumping into the same investments. Maybe the big boys have pressed the buy buttons. Maybe the speculators are buying. Maybe the bottom-fishers are looking for over-sold bargains. Whatever the case, it really doesn't matter. I follow their lead.

There are exceptions, of course, and I don't always use the 10% and 3% rules if I believe interest rates are on the upswing. Even if the numbers are lower, they will tend to go even lower with higher rates. And if I occasionally miss an opportunity, that's fine, because I'd rather remain on the sidelines until the storm has passed.

It's obvious by now that I don't like rising interest rates, but, as I just said, there are exceptions. Precious-metal or foreign funds could do well despite rising North American rates, and I've capitalized on both.

After taking a position in a fund, the cut-loss rule then comes into play. After taking a 9% hit on the chin before selling a resource-based fund during the Gulf War, I learned to stay with the cut-loss. Losing is far more painful than not making, and I won't make that mistake again. You'll find that you will actually learn more from your losses than you do from your gains.

I'm a strong believer in staying diversified, but I don't invest in any more than four funds at a time. Even with the 1991 resource-fund loss, the gains in my other funds more than offset that loss.

I don't like balanced and dividend funds. These funds are generally fine for a lower, steadier rate of return, but I like a little more volatility because it gives me more opportunity. Yes, I am a conservative investor, but I don't consider volatile funds to be high-risk because I buy them only when they're on the upswing.

Specialty funds are normally the most volatile. Their share prices can fall for months, then skyrocket for only a few weeks, and then begin another descent. These funds are commonly driven by higher emotion and expectation. Along with the buy-lower strategy, I also try to determine if the factors influencing these funds are favorable. For example, a rising oil price would benefit the resource fund when it's loaded with oil and gas companies. And with the precious metal fund, I look for the bad news that the "gold bugs" like, such as inflation, currency problems or political instability, which usually drive up the price of the shiny stuff.

Real estate funds, in general, aren't on my shopping list, especially when they contain commercial property. There's no real way to peg how the property is performing, which creates too much uncertainty for this investor. As well, I've heard too many times about major developers and real estate companies going under.

Foreign funds carry more potential when the Canadian dollar is falling, so I like to get my capital out of Canada during dollar declines (The dollar is more likely to fall when it's at a high point). I rather like a falling Canadian dollar because it gives me another way to make money. In fact, many funds do better with a falling Canadian dollar due to the foreign investments in the funds.

If there's a negative to investing within an RRSP, it's the foreign content rule that limits foreign investing to only 20% of your portfolio (There are some exceptions. See Appendix for further details). Some foreign markets can really move in a hurry, particularly when the big boys like them. Oh well, can't have everything.

One thing I believe is that the big boys like to invest in countries whose currencies are expected to rise. With exchange rates it makes them more money. So investing in countries whose currency has fallen and is recovering is often a good strategy. Have I said something like that before?

The mortgage fund, which pays reasonable interest, serves as a base to my portfolio when interest rates are stable. One point with these funds is that their share price reflects mortgage rates, which normally are determined **after** interest rates are set. The delay often lets you anticipate changes to mortgage fund share prices. Moving capital into the mortgage fund before mortgage rates are lowered (i.e., after drops in the Bank of Canada rate), is a way to make a gain. **However,** I have found that when interest rates are falling, the other markets are inclined to do just as well anyway. When the Bank of Canada rate is rising, I switch into the T-Bill fund before mortgage rates go up.

Putting it together:

1. When interest rates are expected to rise, my capital is in the T-Bill fund, unless specific conditions (mentioned in my approach) would make a specialty or foreign fund attractive despite the higher rates. If so, then up to 30% of my portfolio goes into that fund, while the other 70% remains and earns interest in the T-Bill fund.

2. When interest rates are not expected to rise, my capital is broken into four equal amounts. I put 25% into the mortgage fund and the other 75% into the three funds that look the best (If a fund has foreign content restrictions, then only 20% goes into it while 30% goes into another fund). I then watch the numbers. When a fund has dropped between 3% and 5% from its high, the cut-loss kicks in and I switch the money out of that fund and into another one that's recovering. If no funds look attractive, then the money goes into the mortgage

fund with the other 25% leg until an opportunity presents itself.

3. When interest rates change direction to the upside, I sell the funds that will be negatively affected. In effect, I go back to #1 and wait to start over with #2.

Portions of my capital are always earning interest. I prefer the mortgage fund over the bond fund because its share price is more predictable and steady. When buying into the more-volatile funds, I limit my capital to no more than a third. That ensures a diversified portfolio. The mortgage and T-Bill funds are the only funds that do at times hold a higher percentage of my capital (which is still working when not in the markets).

One thing to watch out for is over-switching. You can end up spinning your wheels. I admit to being a little impatient at times, and it usually costs me, especially when I look too much at the short-term. Investing requires patience and my system does not require a lot of switching. You won't be able to earn high rates all the time and sometimes you'll miss opportunities. Such is the case when I avoid funds that are higher but continue to rise. I just don't like buying when there's less likelihood of being correct. And lots of opportunities will come later anyway. Invariably, when I break my rules by chasing all of the winners or by feeding more capital into a rising fund, I lose more than I gain. Greed reduces diversification and increases risk with less upside potential — an overall sucker's bet! (I've learned that, too).

However, on occasion, I will sell a fund before the cut-loss and move into one that is breaking out of its price range. For example, a fund that has been doing nothing for a long time and then starts to rise will often turn out to be a good performer.

Recording the mutual fund share prices is my key to maintaining control. I generally know what the share prices will be before I buy or sell. I always know how much capital is in what fund, and how it's performing. There's never any uncertainty and I don't use a computer. Whenever I switch funds, I circle the numbers affected, receive a confirming statement within a week and double-check the numbers.

My neighbor asked me if I'm on the sidelines a lot since I always sell at the hint of rising interest rates. I replied no, because sometimes a specific market is still doing fine, but moreso because of how interest rates trend.

Even if the longer-term view for interest rates is up, they'll still trend lower for up to several months or more at a stretch. The markets recover during these periods of reprieve, and they then start to rise until the next rate increase. These are excellent times to buy. These periods of reprieve are sometimes an actual change in direction.

Determining when to get back into the markets after interest-rate rises is often done after the stock or bond fund has recovered 3% from a low point. It sometimes takes a gut feeling, but when the numbers are lower, the decisions are easier.

Most of my decisions are made by just following the numbers, but newspapers and newscasts help my keep on top of things, particularly interest-rate direction. The news will sometimes let me act ahead of time. I also look at the semi-annual fund reports, more of an interest than anything else.

After hearing what strategy I use, a friend said I was like a mouse in a large barn, moving around from bin to bin, eating whatever grain looks best at the time, and getting fatter in the process. Perhaps this analogy gives you a picture of my method, but it isn't totally accurate. Imagine instead four mice, who represent diversification. They help each other look for the best food in case one comes across an empty bin (a losing fund), and they go back to their nest (a T-Bill fund) when they hear a large noise (rising interest rates). Mind you, all four mice do get fat (a higher rate of return) by grabbing a grain here and a grain there, and then resting (in the T-Bill fund) in between.

In a nutshell, that's my 17% plan, summarized in a few pages. It sure isn't complicated or difficult to manage and it can be done by almost everyone. My 17% rate of return has been achieved through one of the worst economic times in Canadian history and in spite of starting at one of the worst possible times — when interest rates were climbing and just before The Crash of 87. In addition, I originally misunderstood how some things work and have made some blunders.

Overall, my system enhances rates of returns with minimal risk through a diversified, high-probability approach. You can get a similar — or higher rate of return — by investing in only one fund at a time. But there's generally higher risk with that strategy. I much prefer the safer, steadier route. My highest quarterly gain was 15.6%. There have been only two quarters in which my plan has had a loss, and both losses were minuscule — less than one-half of one per cent. And even when markets took a drubbing in the first six months of 1994, my portfolio gained 9%.

My plan is working, because the money in my PLAN is working.

Plan Summary:

- Invest in one institution's mutual funds, which have daily, no-cost switching privileges.

- Record the funds' share prices and the Bank of Canada rate.

- When to buy:
  When interest rates are stable or falling.
  When funds are recovering.
  When funds are breaking out of price ranges.

- When to sell:
  When interest rates are expected to rise.
  When the cut-loss kicks in.

- Particulars:
  Invest in up to four funds at a time.
  Limit capital going into a volatile fund.
  Wait for the opportunities.

SHARE PRICE FORM

(Sample)

Date	Bank Rate	T-Bill	Mortgage	Bond	Cdn. Equity	Resource	Precious Metal	Asia
Nov 6	5.72	10.00	11.45	9.20	13.50	8.15	14.60	7.10
Nov 7	5.72	10.00	11.45	9.22	13.54	8.20	14.55	7.12
Nov 8	5.72	10.00	11.45	9.21	13.49	8.21	14.56	7.19
Nov 9	5.72	10.00	11.46	9.19	13.45	8.24	14.45	7.18

IT'S YOUR TURN

Through the book, I've guided you through the three steps of earning a higher rate of return — understand the investment, use proven principles, and application.

The next step is for you to make informed decisions and get a higher rate of return yourself. To do so, you first need to review what rate of return you are actually receiving. The answer could come as a real shocker if you haven't been keeping track.

If you find your money is growing far slower than you thought, start looking for ways to improve. For example, are you paying excessive charges when there are ways to avoid them? Are you receiving value? Should you be changing your investments every so often? Are you over-diversified and spread too thin? ARE YOU IN CONTROL?

The Webster Dictionary defines an investor as "One who spends money or capital in expectation of profitable return." Most people are investors — whether or not the investments they buy are guaranteed. What sets investors apart, however, is their ability to accept risk. You may have absolutely no tolerance to accept anything other than guaranteed investments. That's not bad or wrong! Understanding that you're a low-risk investor is far better than buying something you'll worry about. Making or losing money is hardly worth jeopardizing your health or peace of mind.

Your risk tolerance level is an issue to address in terms of what investments you are going to buy, and the strategies you use. How well do you know yourself? How much risk can you absorb? Can you take the odd loss? You'll get to know yourself better after a small loss. And as I said earlier, if you can't take a small loss, chances are you'll take a large one.

My own tolerance level is exceeded when I put too much capital — i.e. more than a third — into the more volatile funds, so I don't do it! Experience will help determine your individual risk level, and with it, you can take measures to find a balance that lets you handle the small, short-term price movements without getting too excited. If you ever find yourself worrying about your investments, then it may be best to rearrange your portfolio into one that's more suitable.

Spreading your money around and dealing with several institutions at once is another way to diversify. You can have as many RRSPs and use as many institutions as you want, although the more you have, the harder it is to maintain control. Again, it depends on your own preferences and comfort levels. I've never found the need to diversify with more than one institution, understanding that the assets of a mutual fund are kept separate from the institution and are protected, so to speak, by their underlying value.

Maybe it's time to review and change the financial institution you use. Maybe your institution no longer suits, and maybe you're doing business there because you "always have." Perhaps there are restrictions or rules that are hindering your investing, and maybe your investments are below average in terms of rates of returns. Transferring your RRSP — or just a part of it, if you want — to another institution can be done as easily as signing your name on form T2033. It's called a direct transfer, issued by the newly chosen institution without any tax considerations. If you do decide to change institutions, determine the charges and whether or not there are any other considerations beforehand. The penalties may be overly severe in some cases.

Some investors have told me that I could earn a higher rate of return in a self-directed RRSP in which I could access other mutual funds or even individual stocks or bonds. Their reasoning is that with more choice, there's more opportunity. That is correct, **but,** my goal is to earn at least 15% per year in a low-risk, uncomplicated environment. So there's no reason to change what I'm doing.

I mentioned earlier that I didn't like self-directed RRSPs, basically because they don't make investing easy enough for me. This bias is not meant to preclude you from having a good look at a self-directed plan, should you have higher goals and the time and ability to manage one. Being able to choose other funds and/or individual stocks and bonds will give you more potential, even with the higher costs.

It's possible to put a mortgage (even your own) into a self-directed RRSP. I think the costs alone generally makes this a poor strategy. And unless interest rates are sky high, only an average rate of return will be realized.

Exercise caution if you do want to buy individual stocks. It's tough to win when you're competing against the professionals who can move in and out of stocks quickly and with tons of money. It would be unfortunate, to say the least, if you bought shares right before someone started to unload millions of them. It's not funny losing your breath when you lose your shirt. Also, recognize the fact that the stock price has to rise up to 10% just to pay the costs before any profit is made. Lastly, remember you need an actual buyer to sell your stock, and it's often the buyer that determines its price (unlike mutual funds which are based on closing values). The thought of owning a stock that nobody wants makes me shudder. Perhaps I'm a little negative on individual stocks because they carry too much risk for me. But, we all have our own comfort zones.

Maybe you'll always want to use a financial planner or investment counsellor to help you, even if there are extra costs and fees. That's fine. Your investment program is too important to take any chances with. And you can have an advisor without giving up control. I've met a few bad apples in the industry, but it's not my intent to paint all of the advisors with the same brush. Find a sincere, independent one.

An independent advisor not getting paid for selling specific investments is, arguably, the best to ensure unbiased information. Find one who pays attention to future trends that can help you adjust your portfolio accordingly. Have a look at the institutions that are now specializing in more short-term mutual fund investing. Their expertise in particular can be well worth the costs. I firmly believe you'll receive the absolute best advice from people with a successful track record — those who have both made money and kept it.

For novice mutual fund investors, consider taking a trial run. Become comfortable with the process first. Refer to Page 27 on how to choose a mutual fund, and do your research. Estimate how much interest you'll earn, find out where the numbers are, and then just pretend to buy. Record the share price(s) of the fund(s) and then follow them, and determine how and why they fluctuate. Factor in the interest you expect to earn and calculate your make-believe rate of return. Compare it with other funds or investments and ask yourself if the choices you made were good ones. Pretend what the consequences would have been if you would have sold or bought other funds in the interim. You'll soon find that by following and working with the numbers, percentages become second nature and you acquire a sixth sense or feeling about the markets themselves. With more experience, you'll begin to look at the numbers without equating them to dollars, and by then, most of the emotion that can come with investing will be gone.

By the end of the year that you reach the age of 71, you have to convert your RRSP. You can either withdraw all of your capital (Not a good idea because it would be fully taxable), buy an annuity which would guarantee a set amount of money each year, or convert your plan to a

Registered Retirement Income Fund (RRIF). Essentially, you manage a RRIF the same as an RRSP, except that each year a minimum amount of money has to be withdrawn. The main benefit with the RRIF is that you retain control of your capital, and you can pass on any remaining capital to your beneficiary — for ***your plan*** to continue.

Ultimately, your investment program and the decisions you make regarding it are your own. I've shown you a way to get a higher rate of return with lower risk, simply by continually buying lower and protecting. You can use my method or adapt it in some fashion. Set your own parameters or find a system that better suits your personality. I know an older couple, for example, that always put their money into the T-Bill fund when travelling because they don't want to follow their funds when they're on the road.

Your rate of return depends on the person you see in the mirror. While I had very little to go by when I first started, you now have the benefit of "no bull" information and experience. But, no matter how confident I am that my system works, the next step is yours to take. SO TAKE IT! You may not only have a fear of failing, but you may also have a fear of being successful. GET OVER THE FEAR AND BE A WINNER INSTEAD! It surely can happen to you, and I would be only too happy to hear that your plan was even better than mine.

The material presented in this book, will, at the very least, help you become better informed, even if you choose not to invest in the same way. Such being the case, I will have considered the book a success. The Investment Funds Institute of Canada (the mutual fund industry's trade association), was, at time of publishing, working on ways to better regulate the mutual fund industry. It's recognized that the consumer is not always being wholly informed.

I saw a lot of funny looks on people's faces when I said I was writing a book. They couldn't understand how a guy my age (39) didn't have to work. When I was a kid, I was fortunate my parents advised me to always save a little for a rainy day. I grew up with the edict, stayed with it, and then started to earn a higher rate of return on the savings. By switching my funds every so often, I was able to switch careers and start doing what I like (My brother Larry is in the same position, and my younger brother Terry is next).

Take my word for it: An RRSP with a higher rate of return really does give you a way to be financially free, rather easily, and in a relatively short period of time. It's worth any effort or sacrifice that you make. While there are few guarantees in life, I do guarantee you'll never regret having *"a plan."* Once again, take control, develop your edge, and all the best in achieving your financial goals.

Create a system, or be enslaved
by someone else's.

William Blake

APPENDIX

Annuity - A contract you buy that pays a fixed amount of income for life.

Bear Market - A market that is trending down.

Bonds are contracts where a borrower promises to pay money back at a certain interest rate for a defined period of time. Government and Corporate bonds are bought and sold in the bond market.

Bull Market - A market that is trending up.

Capital gains is the term given for the profit from an investment that has appreciated in value. Think of an apartment building that rises in price. The price increase is called a capital gain.

Closed-end mutual funds are less common, and different than the open-ended ones described in the book. Closed-ended funds issue only a limited number of shares which are usually traded on stock exchanges.

Currency is the money used by a particular country, such as the Canadian Dollar, the British Pound or the Japanese Yen. Unless otherwise specified, the mutual funds and financial markets that I refer to are Canadian.

Currency factor applies to those investments in mutual funds that are denominated in foreign dollars. A falling Canadian dollar raises their value. Not all foreign mutual funds are denominated in foreign dollars.

Derivative investments are sometimes used by fund managers to complement their funds. They are your regular investments but they are bought and sold in different ways (i.e. futures, options, swaps, forwards and hedging). There's some debate about the use of these products. My opinion: Don't worry about what the fund manager is doing. Be more concerned with how the fund itself is doing, and make decisions accordingly.

Dividends are interest payments to shareholders.

Distributions are fund payouts to the shareholders. They are normally related to interest or capital gains. Sometimes they affect the share price, other times they don't. Some mortgage and bond funds, for example, reflect the earned interest in the share price; then on valuation day, the interest is paid, which lowers the price. Other mortgage and bond funds will keep the interest separate from the share price, keeping the share price constant when the interest is paid.

Elephants never forget.

Foreign Content Rules - As of January 1994, you are allowed to invest 20% of the value of your RRSP in foreign investments. There are now some foreign mutual funds that are not considered to be foreign content. These funds more or less buy Canadian investments which are then used or leveraged to buy foreign investments. Nonetheless, there is no 20% investing limit with these funds, giving you better access to the foreign markets within your RRSP.

GICs are guaranteed investment certificates. They pay interest for a set period of time and are insured by Canada Deposit Insurance Corporation (CDIC) for up to $60,000.

Hedge fund - Another mutual fund you might run into. Not very common, but they contain a lot of derivative products (See derivatives).

Inflation rate is the standard used to measure rising prices.

Interest rate - the cost of money.

Interest to be received from a mutual fund:
To approximate how much interest a fund will pay, find out what interest the fund payed the previous year. If interest rates have been stable in the interim, the interest you'll receive will be close to the same. Some financial institutions now have computer models that are able to tell you how much interest will be payed.

Mortgages are contracts where a borrower promises to pay money back at a certain interest rate for a defined period of time with property used for collateral.

Mutual fund - an investment fund, or a fund with investments in it, mutually owned by the shareholders.

Net Asset Value Per Share (The fund's share price):
The NAVPS is the net asset value of the investments divided by the number of outstanding shares.

When a mutual fund is valued, all of the investments in the fund are valued, or priced, based on the closing prices in the financial markets. On valuation day, the current value of each investment is calculated and totalled. That total value (less expenses) is then divided by the total number of outstanding shares, which gives you the fund's current share price. If the Net Asset Value of a fund is $1,000,000, for example, and there are 200,000 outstanding shares, then the NAVPS or share price is $5 ($1,000,000 divided by 200,000)

The original size of the share price doesn't affect gains or losses. With a 15% gain, for example, a $4.00 price will rise to $4.60, while a $40.00 price will rise to $46.00. At first glance, you may think there's more money being made with the fund with the higher share price. But with the higher share price, you would have originally purchased 10 times fewer shares. Owning fewer shares at a larger share price, or owning more shares at a smaller share price, will produce the same result.

Pension plan - A plan that makes regular payments based on prior service and/or contributions.

Percentages measure performance and fluctuations better than just sticking with the actual numbers. A price that rises 10 cents from a dollar, for example, is a better gain than one that rises 10 cents from five dollars.

To calculate a percentage, multiply the percentage rate by the number and divide by 100. For example, 30 per cent of 500 is 30 x 500 divided by 100, which comes to 150 (If you use a calculator, go 30 x 500 and then hit the per cent sign).

To calculate a percentage gain or loss, take "the difference," divide it by the starting point and then multiply by 100 (Using the per cent sign on the calculator is the same as multiplying by 100 in this case). Suppose, for example, a share price rises from $4.50 to $4.75.

- the difference is $.25 ($4.75 - $4.50)
- the starting point is $4.50.
- the percentage gain is .25 divided by $4.50 x 100, or 5.55%.

Rates of Return - Your rate of return is the difference between a mutual fund's rate of return, and your costs to invest. The higher the rate of return and the less your costs, the better. A fund that earns 12%, for example, with no extra charges, is superior to one that earns 15% with a 5% load fee.

To calculate your yearly rate of return, take how much money you made over the year, (exclude any monthly contributions made) divide that figure by the amount of money you had at the beginning of the year, and then multiply the answer by 100.

To calculate your past compounded yearly rate of return, combine your yearly rates of return and then divide that figure by the number of years being considered.

Increasing rates of return is achieved by keeping profits and minimizing losses and expenses.

To calculate a fund's yearly rate of return (If it's not in the prospectus), get the yearly starting and finishing share prices, and the distributions per share earned. Take the difference between the two share prices, add in any distributions per share earned, divide your answer by the starting share price, and then multiply by 100.

Registered Retirement Savings Plan (RRSP) - A plan that gives you a tax deduction when you contribute, and lets money compound tax-free until withdrawals are made.

Registered Retirement Income Fund (RRIF) - An extension of an RRSP, except that minimum withdrawals are made yearly. Those withdrawals are taxable. (A RRIF is like an RRSP in reverse).

RISK with a mutual fund generally refers to the volatility of the fund's share price. To calculate volatility mathematically, take the difference between the fund's yearly high and low share prices, divide the answer by the low share price, and then multiply by 100 for the percentage. If the high share price is $5.00 and the low is $4.00, you have a 25% variation ($1 divided by $4 x 100). To me, that means a fund could gain or lose about 25% a year (Not taking distributions into account). Risk with a new mutual fund is more difficult to analyze.

Self-directed RRSP - An RRSP that lets you invest in a variety of investments, including individual stocks, bonds, T-Bills, mutual funds and term deposits. It also enables you to buy all of these investments from a variety of institutions, through a single institution.

Share Value - The overall value of your shares is the total number of shares you own, multiplied by the current share price.

Stocks or shares are pieces of paper that represent a form of ownership. Some pay dividends, others don't. The stock market determines their value.

Switching mutual funds or other investments within your RRSP does not affect the status of your RRSP (There aren't any tax considerations until you remove money from your plan).

Treasury Bills are like GICs except they are backed by the government rather than being insured by Canada Deposit Insurance Corporation.

Valuation day - When a mutual fund is valued; when a fund's share price is calculated; when you can buy or sell shares of a fund.